Puzzle Play

Alien adventure

written & illustrated
by Kia Marie Hunt

Published by Collins
An imprint of HarperCollins Publishers
HarperCollins Publishers
Westerhill Road
Bishopbriggs
Glasgow G64 2QT

www.harpercollins.co.uk

HarperCollins Publishers
Macken House,
39/40 Mayor Street Upper,
Dublin 1, Ireland
D01 C9W8

10 9 8 7 6 5 4 3 2 1

ISBN 978-0-00-866594-4

Printed and bound in India

A catalogue record for this book is available from the British Library.

Publisher: Michelle l'Anson
Author and Illustrator: Kia Marie Hunt
Project Manager: Sarah Woods
Designer: Kevin Robbins

Puzzle Play

Alien adventure

written & illustrated
by Kia Marie Hunt

Your Alien adventure starts here!

On strange planets, in faraway galaxies there are aliens waiting for you, aliens playing games, aliens who love puzzles and aliens who need your help!

Come along and explore outer space. Play with the aliens, solve fun puzzles and collect clues along the way!

Things you'll need:

- ◎ This book
- ◎ Some pens, pencils or crayons
- ◎ Your amazing brain

That's it!

(You can colour in any bits of this book!)

Always look out for this arrow:

This means you've found a clue.

Write down all the clues you find on page 38.

Can you fly your rocket through the galaxy maze all the way to the planet?

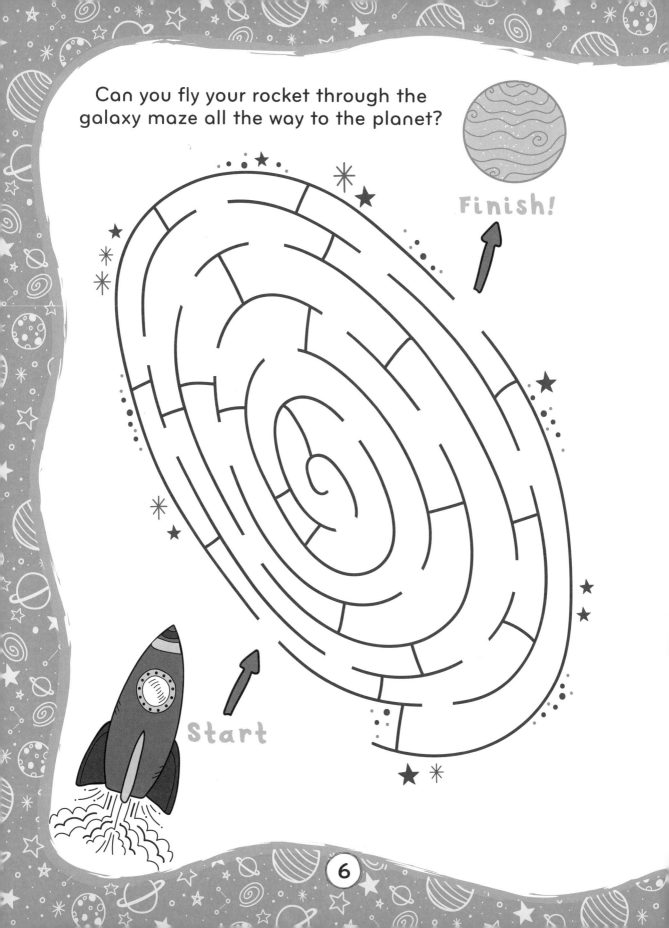

Finish!

Start

Use the pictures in the key below to fill in the missing letters and find the name of this new planet.

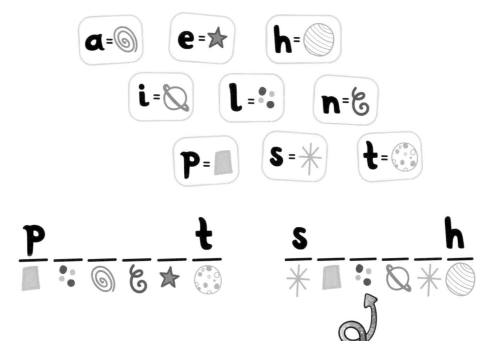

a = ⊚   e = ★   h = ◯

i = ⊘   l = ∴   n = ℰ

p = ▱   s = ✳   t = ◌

P _ _ _ t   s _ _ _ _ h
▱ ∴ ⊚ ℰ ★ ◌   ✳ ▱ ∴ ⊘ ✳ ◯

When you see an arrow like this, write the letter it is pointing to in the key on page 38.

Hi! My name is shloop. welcome to my planet!

On the strange new planet, you meet a friendly alien with a funny name!

Shloop is an alien that can change colour
to blend into any place she explores!

Can you finish colouring in this picture
of Shloop to match the different backgrounds?

Uh oh...

Shloop was playing hide and seek in the swamp with her babies and can't find them!

Which path takes you to the swamp to look for Shloop's babies? Write your answer (**a**, **b**, **c** or **d**) in this box:

Oh no, I need your help!

a   b   c   d

The Swamp

The alien swamps on Planet Splish are
very different to the swamps here on Earth.
There are lots of hiding places!

Can you work out the number pattern on each
mushroom? Write the missing number in the empty
shape at the top of each mushroom.

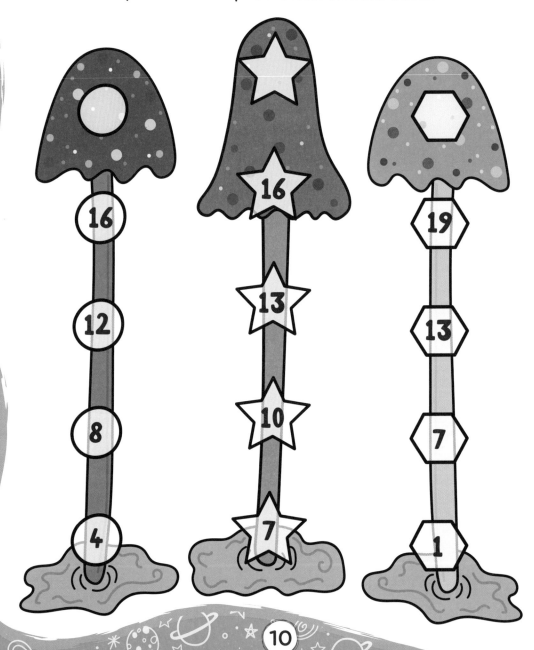

How many of Shloop's babies can you find hiding in this picture of the swamp?

Each one of Shloop's babies has a colour twin, except one. Can you find and circle the odd one out?

Colour in the white babies. They are twins so make them match!

Complete the number problem below each letter. Use the answers to fill in the gaps in the sentence. For example, the number 3 = the letter t.

a
8+1
=

f
4+3
=

h
8−6
=

i
6−1
=

n
9−1
=

o
2+2
=

t
5−2
=3

u
10−4
=

y
8−7
=

My babies are a bit t _ _ _
3 4 4

g _ _ d at playing hide and
4 4

seek! T _ _ _ k _ _ _ for
2 9 8   1 4 6

f _ _ d _ _ g them for me!
5 8   5 8

It's time to fly through space on another adventure to meet a different kind of alien...

The numbers show the order of a repeating pattern of spaceships. Can you complete the line to the finish? You can only move up, down or sideways.

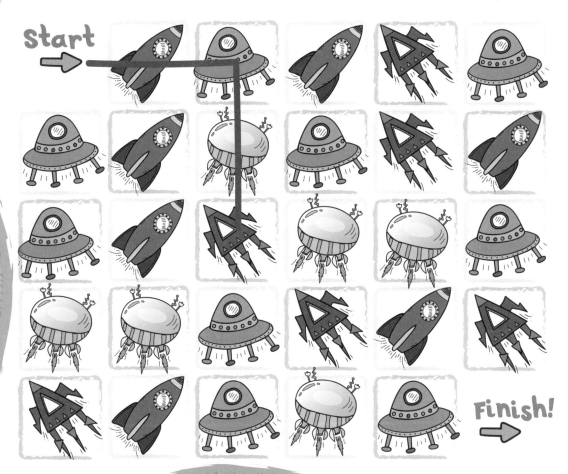

You've safely landed on Planet Pebble!

Which path will take you to meet your new alien pal? Write your answer (**a**, **b**, **c** or **d**) in this box:

a   b   c   d

Hello! My name is Mudd. Nice to meet you!

Oops! I need to give the astronauts a tour of Planet Pebble but I can't find my glasses!

map   tour   space

planet   glasses   astronaut

Can you complete the grid with the words above? Each word is used just once, so cross it off when you place it to help you keep track!

The astronauts have travelled from far and wide to explore Planet Pebble!

Can you spot six differences between these two pictures of the astronauts? Put a circle around each one.

Without my special glasses, I can't see the map!

The astronauts want to go to Pebble Towers, which they can climb up to get a good view of the planet's famous Three Moons.

Can you help Mudd lead the tour through the maze to Pebble Towers?

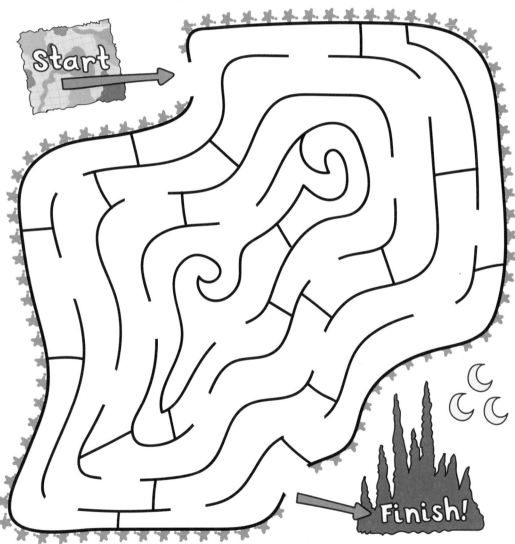

Start

Finish!

Write the letter of the black shape that matches the picture of Pebble Towers.

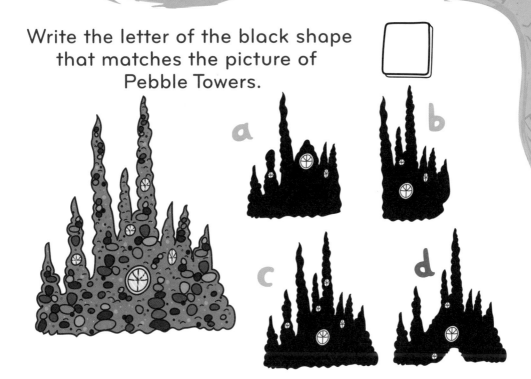

From the top of Pebble Towers, you can see the Three Moons and lots of different planets in the sky!

Complete the number problem in each moon and write your answers into the coloured circles.

10 - 3 =

13 - 5 =

15 - 6 =

Colour in the planets and stars!

Guess what you find at the top of Pebble Towers?
Mudd's glasses! Mudd is very happy you found them.

Can you find the six words
below in the wordsearch?

Words may be hidden across or down.

```
j o l l y r b l
o a w e m h g u
y u p k e i l c
c j v o r b m k
c h e e r f u l
h a p p y l d o
```

cheerful   happy   jolly

joy   luck   merry

Use the pictures in the key below to fill in the missing letters and complete Mudd's message.

a = 🪐   h = ⠓   e = ☆   m = ♪

n = ✦   s = ◎   u = 🪐

WOW!
Look at you!
I've never

◎ ☆ ☆ ✦ a ⠓ 🪐 ♪ 🪐 ✦

UP close
before!

21

Want to play with an alien from another galaxy? Fly through the rocket maze all the way from Planet Pebble to Planet Mist!

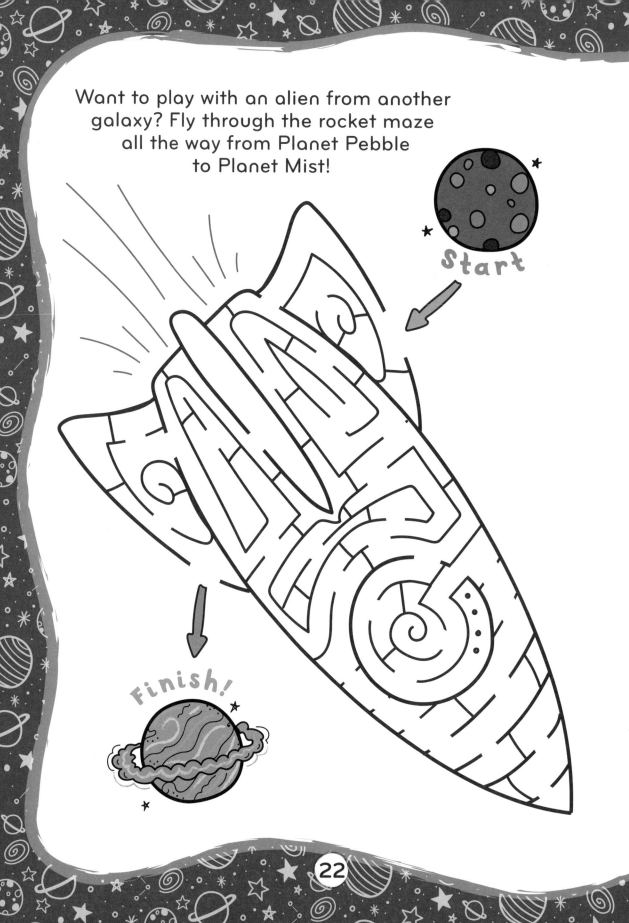

Start

Finish!

This planet is home to floating aliens that look a bit like clouds. They are called Misties.

Each Misty has an identical twin, except one. Can you find and circle the odd one out?

Colour in the white aliens. They are twins so make them match!

On this planet, big storm aliens called Nightmares block the sky and stop the Misties from floating and playing in the sky!

Can you spot six differences between these two pictures of the Nightmares? Put a circle around each one.

Complete the number problem below each letter. Use the answers to fill in the gaps in the sentence. For example, the number 1 = the letter y.

a	b	g	h	l
5+2	4-2	4-1	11-1	3+3
=	=	=	=	=

m	n	r	w	y
10-1	4+4	7-2	10-6	4-3
=	=	=	=	= 1

The _ i _ _ t _ _ _ e s are
   8   3 10   9 7 5

back! Will you help me

_ _ o _   them   _ _ _ y ?
2 6 4   7 4 7 1

For this adventure, you and Rush make your
way to Planet Mist's giant windmill!

Which path will take you to the windmill?
Write your answer
(**a**, **b**, **c** or **d**) in this box:

a   b   c   d

Let's fix the giant windmill and blow the Nightmares away!

Draw the other half of the windmill, then colour it in to make it symmetrical!

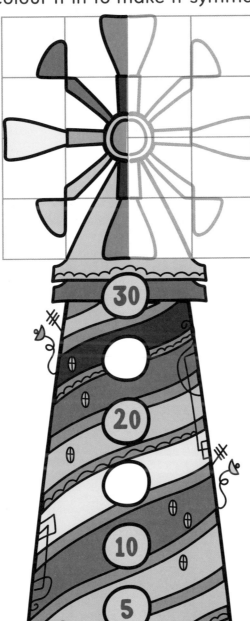

Can you work out the number pattern on the windmill?

Write the missing numbers in the empty circles.

One by one, the giant windmill blows the Nightmares away so the Misties can float and play again!

1   2   3   4

The numbers show the order of a repeating pattern. Can you complete the line to the finish? You can only move up, down or sideways.

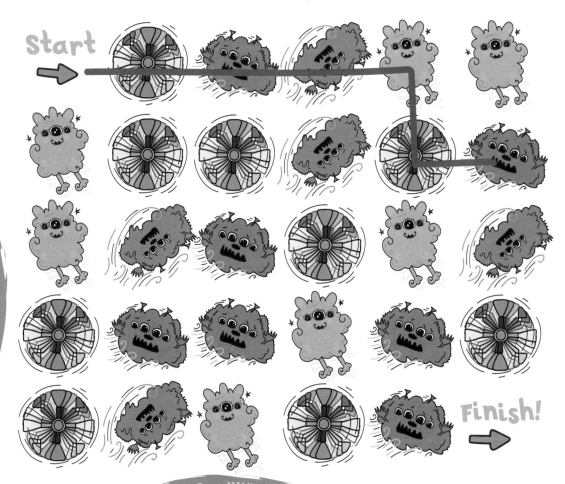

Start

Finish!

3 LETTERS:
yay

Thank you! You are our hero!

4 LETTERS:
hero

6 LETTERS:
aliens
cloudy

8 LETTERS:
windmill

10 LETTERS:
nightmares

Can you complete the grid with the words above? Each word is used just once, so cross it off when you place it to help you keep track!

Thanks!

yay!

Yippee!

Ready for another adventure?
To get to the next planet, join
the dots to complete the picture
of the rocket, then colour it in!

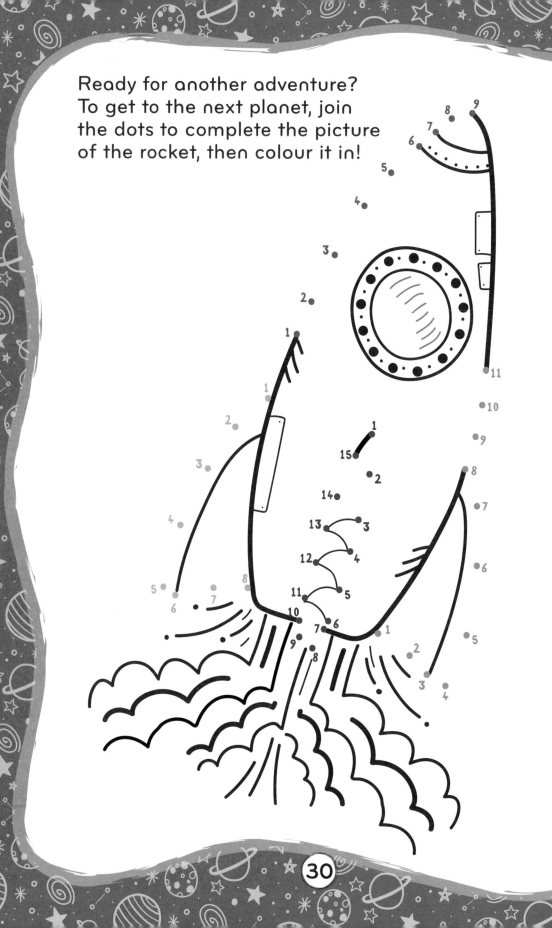

Use the pictures in the key below to fill in the missing letters and find the name of this alien and the planet they live on.

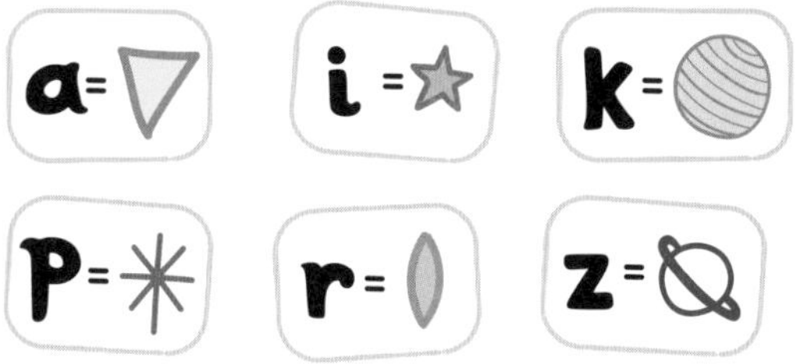

a = ▽ i = ★ k = ⬤

P = ✳ r = ◗ z = 🪐

Hi! My name is
F _ _ _ .
  ★ 🪐 🪐

Welcome to Planet
S _ _ _ _ _ !
  ✳ ▽ ◗ ⬤

31

Fizz is one of many aliens who live here on Planet Spark.

These special aliens have superpowers:
they can create and control fire AND electricity!

How many Spark aliens can you
find hiding in this picture?

Which black shape matches the shape of Fizz the alien?

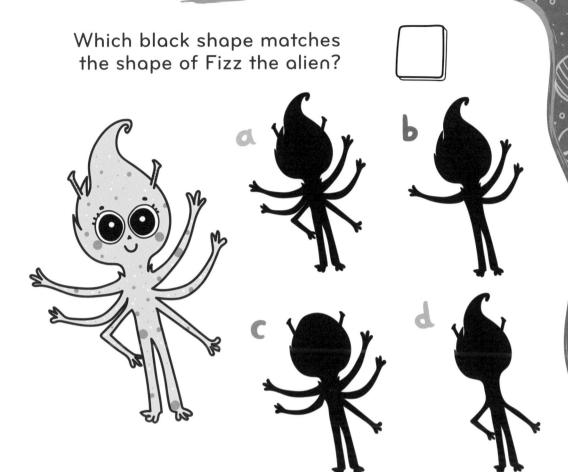

a

b

c

d

Complete the number problem in each flame and write your answers into the coloured circles.

8 - 4 =

9 - 3 =

10 - 2 =

All of the Spark aliens have fiery names!

Can you find the six words
below in the wordsearch?

Words may be hidden across or down.

```
g l q f a i c p
u f l i c k e r
b l a z e j t y
e k c z s n a p
c r a c k l e o
r n i m o z s p
```

Blaze   Crackle   Fizz

Flicker   Pop   Snap

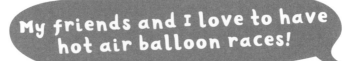

My friends and I love to have hot air balloon races!

The Spark aliens use their flames to power the balloons!

Can you follow the numbers up the balloon trails and work out the number pattern on each one? Write the missing numbers in the empty circles in the balloons.

22
20
18
16

30
40
50

Draw a pattern on the white balloon and colour it in!

9
13
17
21

> ## we have a fun idea!

Can you cross out each letter **Z** and write the letters left over onto the lines below to find out what the Spark aliens would like your help with? Some words have been done for you.

ẉwẓeẓwẓoẓulẓdẓloẓẓvẓetzo
tzrzazvelztozyzozuzr
zgazlzazxyaznzdzzvziszitz
zyozuzrpzlzanzeztz!

w e   w o u l d   l o v e   _ _

_ _ _ _ _   _ _   _ _ _ _

_ _ _ _ _   _ _   _ _ _ _

_ _ _ _   _ _ _ _ _ _ !

Can you lead the alien spaceship
from Planet Spark through the maze
all the way to Earth?

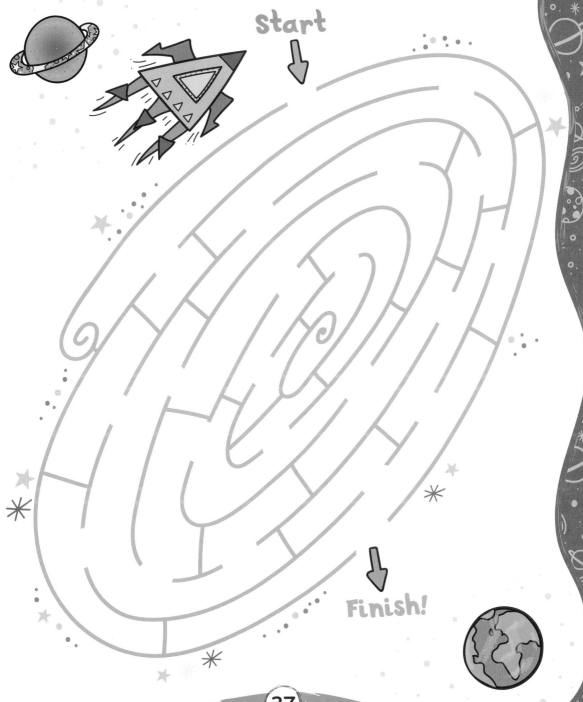

Start

Finish!

Crack the code for a special message...

Look back through the book and collect any letters that have this arrow pointing to them:

These are your clue letters!

Write the missing clue letters into the key below. For example, because you found the letter 'L' on page 7, the letter 'L' is in the '7' box.

l — 7

15

21

26

29

36

Once your key is ready you can use it to fill in the missing letters and reveal our special message!

Did yo_ h_v_
       36   26 21
f_n on yo_r
 36   36
A_i_n A_v_nt_re?
 7 21   15 21 36
W_ sure ha_ fun
 21   15
with yo_! Th_nk_
       36   26 29
for vi_iting and
       29
P__a_e come b_ck
 7 21 29   26
_g_in _oon!
26 26   29

Congratulations! Don't forget to complete your Puzzle Play certificate on Page 47!

Answers

Page 6

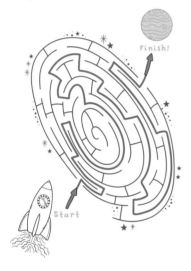

Page 7

planet splish

Page 8

Page 9

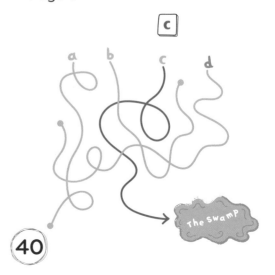

Page 10

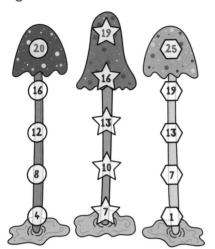

Page 11

How many Baby Shloops can you find hiding in this picture of the swamp? **10**

Page 12

Page 13

a	f	h	i
8+1	4+3	8−6	6−1
=9	=7	=2	=5

n	o	t	u	y
9−1	2+2	5−2	10−4	8−7
=8	=4	=3	=6	=1

My babies are a bit $\underset{3}{t}\underset{4}{o}\underset{4}{o}$

$\underset{4}{g}\underset{4}{o}\underset{}{o}d$ at playing hide and

seek! $\underset{2}{T}\underset{9}{h}\underset{8}{a}\underset{}{n}k$ $\underset{1}{y}\underset{4}{o}\underset{6}{u}$ for

$\underset{5}{f}\underset{8}{i}\underset{}{n}\underset{5}{d}\underset{8}{i}\underset{}{n}g$ them for me!

Page 14

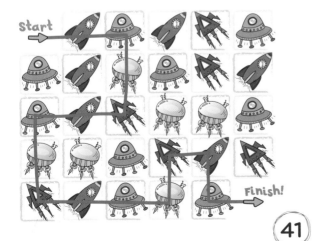

Start

Finish!

(41)

Page 15

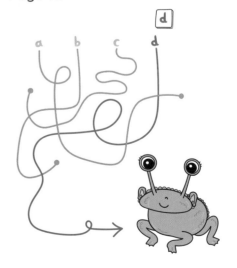

d

a   b   c   d

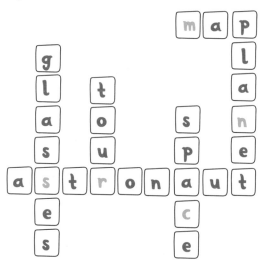

Page 22

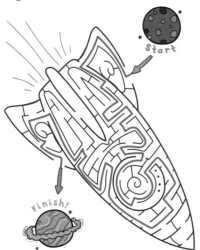

Page 23

Page 24

Page 25

a	b	g	h	l
5+2	4−2	4−1	11−1	3+3
= 7	= 2	= 3	=10	= 6

m	n	r	w	y
10−1	4+4	7−2	10−6	4−3
= 9	= 8	= 5	= 4	= 1

The n i g h t m a r e s are
 8 3 10 9 7 5

back! Will you help me

b l o w them a w a y?
2 6 4   7 4 7 1

Page 26

b

a   b   c   d

Page 27

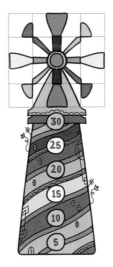

30
25
20
15
10
5

Page 28

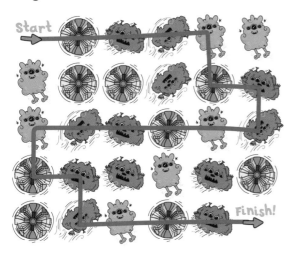

Page 29

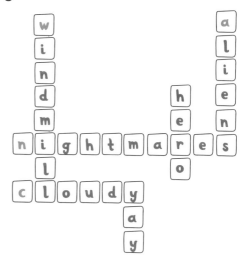

Page 30

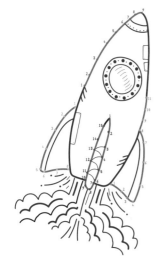

Page 31

Page 32

How many Spark aliens can you find hiding in this picture? **9**

Page 33

Page 34

Page 35

Page 36

We would love to travel to your galaxy and visit your planet!

Page 37

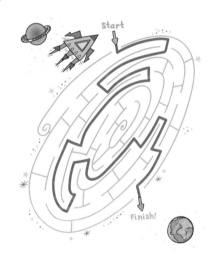

Page 38

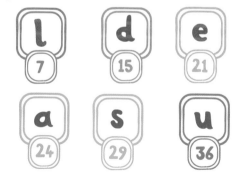

Page 39

Did you have
36 26 21

fun on your
36 36

Alien Adventure?
7 21 15 21 36

We sure had fun
21 15

with you! Thanks
36 26 29

for visiting and
29

Please come back
7 21 29 26

again soon!
26 26 29

Colour in and cut out a Picture of your alien friends!

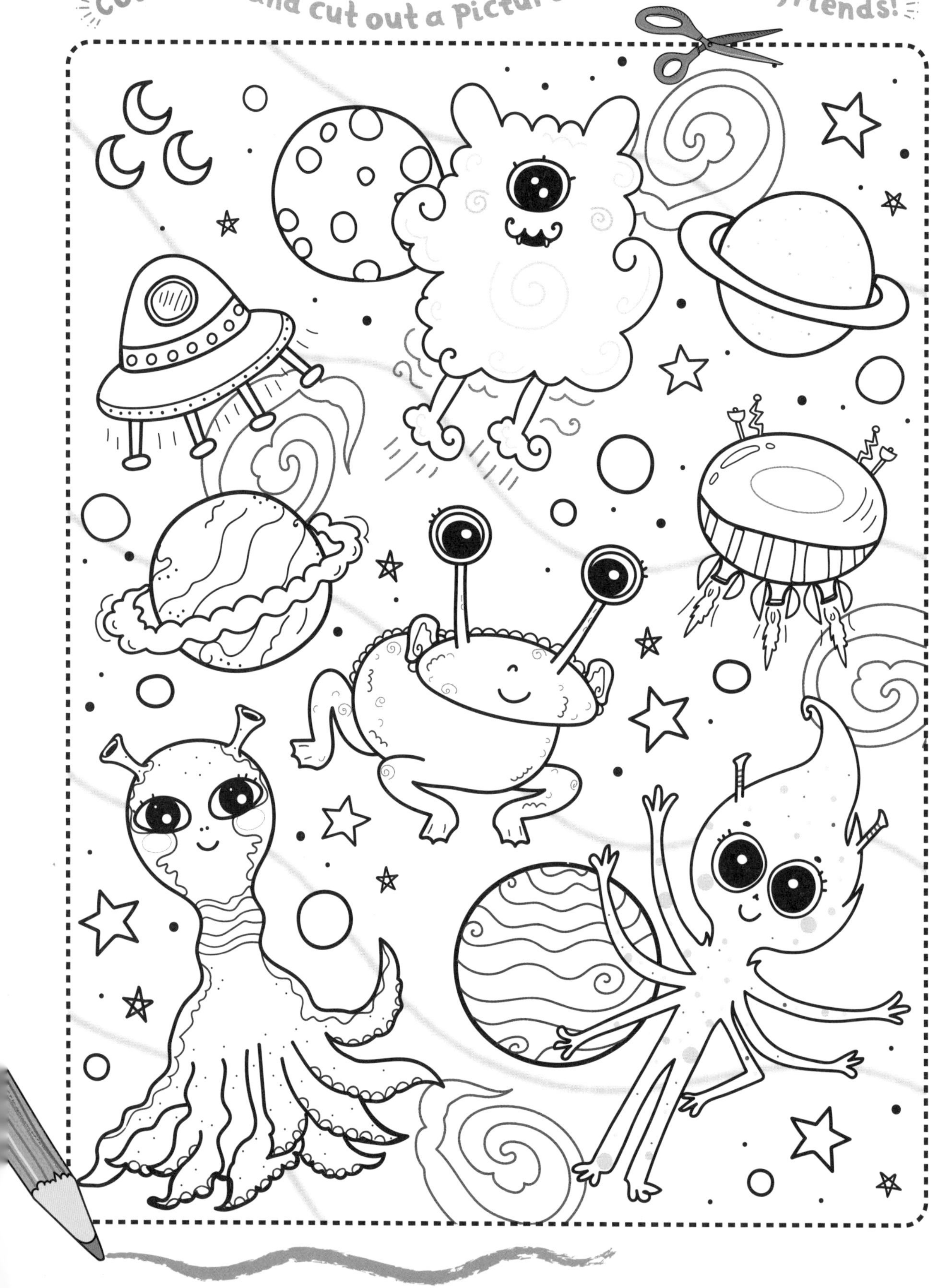

Well done!
This certificate is awarded to:

(your name)

for completing their intergalactic
Puzzle Play
Alien Adventure on:

(the date)

Shloop Mudd Rush Fizz

signed:

(your signature)